YO-EIL-275

Trails of the Farmer's Daughter

By Sandra (Booher) Sturgeon

A Rancho Lazarus Publication
Payson, Arizona

TRAILS OF THE FARMER'S DAUGHTER

Copyright 2013 by Sandra (Booher) Sturgeon

All rights reserved.

Published by Rancho Lazarus Publications
PO Box 2047
Payson AZ 85547

www.rancholazarus.com

ISBN 978-0615624204

First edition May 2013

Printed in the United States of America

Cover Photo— The Author at age 13 on "Star"

Dedicated to my family -- past, present, and future.

Table of Contents

Preface 1
Chapter 1
    Family History 3
Chapter 2
    The Irish Twins 12
Chapter 3
    The Singing Booher Sisters 16
Chapter 4
    Don't Fence Me In 19
Chapter 5
    The Good Ol' Days 28
Chapter 6
    My Awesome Aunties 32
Chapter 7
    Good Night for A Little While 38
Chapter 8
    Fashions and Traditions 42
Family Photo Album 45
Chapter 9
    I'm Gonna Marry That Boy Someday! 55
Chapter 10
    Boy, Oh Boy, Oh Boy, Oh Boy! 62
Chapter 11
    We Always Had Room for One More 69
Chapter 12
    Thank God I Never Made It Past Preschool! 76
Chapter 13
    The Darkest Day, April 22, 2004 82
Chapter 14
    Never Look Back 87
Chapter 15
    A Cold Nose Can Feel So Warm! 92
In Closing 96
An Ending Poem to Ponder 97

Trails of the Farmer's Daughter

Preface

My daughter-in-law, Amy, actually inspired me to begin writing this book. While visiting our home on Conesus Lake in New York, during the summer of 2010, she commented on what a wise and wonderful man my father was, and what a shame that he didn't write a book and share all of his knowledge to be passed on down for generations to come.

After she left, I began thinking about what she had said, and like a lightning bolt it hit me that I was now the oldest living member of our immediate family. It was up to me to hand down any memories or stories that I could recall so that my family would have some knowledge of the past. I began writing the day after she left.

Even though I'm not nearly as creative or full of wisdom as my father was, I would like to share some of the stories and experiences I had while growing up on the farm and moving through life.

I hope that whoever is reading this book will discover some information that they didn't know before and perhaps share a laugh, or a tear, as I did, while writing this book.

It has taken me nearly two years to write this and put it into book format. Today is a very joyous day for me. The date is 11-11-11. It is not only an important day in history, but also my 67th birthday, and today I finished my book! It is ready to go to print. My goal is to have a copy in the hands of each of my children by my 70th birthday. I am not a writer, but everything comes directly from my heart.

Thanks Amy for inspiring me, and happy trails to all.

Sandra Booher Sturgeon
November 11, 2011

Chapter 1

Family History

EVEN THOUGH I'VE NEVER SPENT time tracing our family tree, I did read some interesting facts. Our ancestors were from Niederweningen, Switzerland, which is located about 15 miles from the city of Zurich in a valley between two high hilltops. The valley is called Wehntal, and is one of the prettiest landscapes in the entire Canton of Zurich.

Being that our ancestors spoke German, many misinterpretations were made of the correct spelling of our name by census takers, tax assessors, and record takers. Since 1851, it has been spelled Bucher, Buher, Beuhart, Boer, and Booker. The only place Booher was spelled correctly was on great-grandpa Booher's tombstone in the Montmorenci Cemetery, and on one tax record dated 1858.

Looking back at the occupations of some of our early ancestors, I found that I had one grandfather in Switzerland who rolled tobacco leaves and sold cigars by trade and a Swiss grandmother who was a gingerbread maker.

Due to an economic recession in Switzerland in 1850, my great-great grandfather, Casper Booher, decided to bring his family to America. Before reaching New York City, a son, Philip (my great grandfather) was born on the boat on May 4, 1851.

I am quite envious of my great-great grandparents. After settling in America, they built a log home in 1852 amid a large orchard in Indiana, north of the Tippecanoe-White County Line Road, which is a quarter-mile East of 231 (old Hwy. 53). It has always been my dream to live in a log home.

Casper began farming at this location in 1852. Today, six generations later, our family still farms this land, but the log home is gone. How I wish that it were still there!

When Philip grew up, he fell in love with Hannah Bader and they were married in 1878. She was the neighborhood nurse and always helped when needed.

Philip and Hannah owned one of the only telephones in the area. The Montmorenci merchants would call them to check on the weather in the northern part of the township.

All of the Booher men were farmers. At the time, oats and corn sold for 11 cents a bushel. Philip was a big cattle raiser and was known as the "Cattle King" of the area.

Philip and Hannah reared six children. They all attended Mount Tom School, which was just a short distance up the road from where our farm now stands. During the cold winter months, the Boohers housed some of the teachers in their home so they would not become stranded in the snow. The children would walk to school and on Sundays the entire family would walk to the school again as church was held in that same building. (In 1901 my great-uncle, Jacob Booher, donated a tract of land for the building of the Union Chapel United Brethren Church in Christ.)

In 1924 Philip fell from a manger in the barn and never fully recovered. He died in 1928 at the age of about 77. Hannah had passed away earlier, in 1925, from Trench Mouth.

Philip's brother, Jacob, enlisted in the War of Rebellion (the American Civil War) and, while in the army, he was run over by an army wagon. He never completely recovered from his injuries either.

It was noted that my great-grandfather, Philip, was a thrifty person and believed in anything for the improvement of the community in which he lived.

One of his children, Joseph Booher, was my grandfather. Joseph married Carrie Wettschurack and they were blessed with four children: Mildred, Earl, Ralph, and Dorothy. My father, Ralph Joseph Booher, their third child, was born on October 10, 1912. Ralph married my mother, Doris Isabel Solomon on November 23, 1939.

I remember my dad saying what an unusual day it was. His grandmother Wettschurack had died that week, so they went straight from their noon wedding at Trinity Methodist Church in Lafayette to his grandmother's funeral that same afternoon.

I know very little about my mother's family except that they were quite poor, but proud. Grandpa Ross Solomon died in 1918 of pneumonia at age 29 when my mother was barely three years old, leaving grandma to rear three young children. Grandma took in ironings and my mother and her brothers ran a paper route.

Grandpa Ross & Grandma Cora Solomon, with their children Woody, Isabel, and Bob, 1916

Mother was always quite proud of the fact that she was a registered nurse. It was quite an accomplishment back in those days, and she totally funded her own way through nurse's training.

My mother was always quite frail and suffered many bouts of pneumonia and lung diseases in her latter years. She developed septicemia shortly before her death. Dementia set in as well as a few mini-strokes. We were forced to move her to a nursing home a year before her death. That was the only time I had ever seen my dad cry. Moving my parents off the farm was one of the hardest things I've ever done. Mother eventually succumbed to a stroke on May 19, 2002 at the age of 87.

Dad's last year on the farm, Oct. 2002. Putting the 1939 Silver King to rest. Foreground L-R Dad and Grandson A.J. who now farms the land & great grandchildren Evan (on top), J Dan (at wheel), Adam (L) and Allison.

Dad was able to remain on the farm with minimal assistance until he reached 90 years of age. Even though we had taken away his car, a neighbor reportedly saw him trying to ride to town on his tractor! He was a great lover of the land and it was very difficult to move him away from the only life he had known. A year after mother had passed away, dad fell in the home and so, for his own safety, we moved him into an assisted living facility. Dad was so cooperative and never complained. As I said in my eulogy at his funeral, "He was a perfect 10!"

We laid dad to rest on March 10, 2004 following a losing battle with pneumonia. He was anxious to be with mother. They had been married 67 years when mother passed away. Dad was 91 years old at his death.

After their passing, my mother's nurse's uniform was placed on display in the Tippecanoe County Historical Museum. Her class of four students was the last to graduate from the Lafayette Home Hospital School of Nursing.

Display of mom's nurse's uniform and diploma at the Tippecanoe County Historical Museum.

Shortly thereafter, we were asked to set up a display in the museum honoring my father. He was a very successful farmer in Tippecanoe County. He had invented a tandem tractor hook-up with his very creative mind, so we proudly set up a display in his honor as well.

Ralph Booher on tractor, west of the house. This is the tandem tractor hook-up he created. Circa 1960.

Between the stamina of the Solomons and the wealth and knowledge of the Boohers, I feel truly blessed to be a branch on these family trees.

I love to write poems and express myself through poetry. The day after each of my parents' deaths, I sat down and wrote a poem from my heart and read it at their funerals. It was a small tribute to them for all that they had done for me.

A Tribute to our Mother

DORIS ISABELLE BOOHER

1916-2003

Although your journey here is over
And we now may feel alone,
We must rejoice in knowing
That you're finally going home.

Letting go is hard to do
Whenever loved ones die;
But now another angel
Is watching from the sky.

Through the years your guidance
Has influenced all we do;
And all the good that we do now
Are values learned from you.

You taught us how to love our friends
And also how to care;
And how to comfort those in need
Just by being there.

And in the end we made it through
Each long and difficult day;
Just because when we were young
You taught us how to pray.

You gave us life, you gave us faith
You loved us like no other;
For all you've done, and what we've become
We owe to you, dear Mother.

Love and Thank You.

~ A Tribute to Our Dad ~

Ralph J. Booher

1912 – 2004

~ The Legendary Farmer ~

Amidst the shocks of wheat and oats and golden fields of corn,
The world rejoices for unto us a little child is born.
A second boy for Joe & Carrie, Ralph will be his name,
And unknowingly to all of us, we'll never be the same.

A gentleman, a Christian man, with abundant patience galore,
The kind of father any child would worship and adore.
We stood upon this solid rock, with standards he set high,
He was a great example for us to all live by.

Even though modern technology would try to change his ways,
He'd love to tell you stories about the good old days.
He remembered horse drawn buggies & lanterns in the night,
He remembered Charles Lindberg and witnessing the first space flight.

He was a book of knowledge, he was a wealth of advice,
He was never in a hurry, and he was always nice.
We would say, "How are you doing? Are you having any pain?"
And sweetly he would answer, "I really can't complain!"

He was the gentle hand that guided us,
Our friend along the way.
The reason why we had the strength,
To face another day.

Working in the toolshed, repairing machinery at night,
A perfectionist working diligently until he got it right.
I don't believe there was a task this man's hands could not do,
Dear Jesus, the carpenter, he was so much like You.

But today the rooster was not crowing as the sun rose on the farm,
But in the heavens, Mom and Dad were walking arm in arm.
Though memories will sustain us, the farm will never be the same,
And tears will fall upon the fields, every time it rains.

He loved the farm, the planted fields, and working up the sod,
And when he brought the harvest in, he gave all praise to God.
But like the harvest in the fall, he reaped from seeds he'd sown,
His life completed its cycle, and the master called him home.

Who was this man we spoke about?
Who was this King of Men?
We knew him well, we called him Dad,
He was a perfect – 10!

Chapter 2

The Irish Twins

It's 5:30 A.M. on the farm of Ralph and Isabel Booher located on the Tippecanoe-White County Line Road in northern Shelby Township. The roosters are crowing to announce the arrival of a new farmer's daughter, soon to be named Sandra Sue Booher. It is November 11, 1944, better known then as Armistice Day.

It has been a very eventful year for the Booher family as they had already welcomed another baby girl, Linda Lou, on January 11, exactly 10 months earlier. Wow! Two babies in 1944!

Sometime later they were told that they were parents of Irish Twins, meaning you have two children born in the same year.

Apparently our mother took this twin thing way "two" seriously, as from that day forward she always dressed us alike, gave us identical Christmas gifts, and many times for birthdays we would each get a gift so that we would have matching outfits. That part was pretty cool!

Mother was a good seamstress and would make a lot of identical clothes for us to wear to school. She always raised chickens and Kissell's Hatchery and Feed Store would deliver egg mash in printed cotton 50-pound bags. She would take the old gunnysack and beat it on the back fence until all the dust from the chicken feed disappeared. Then she would run the sack through the old wringer washing machine down in the basement and then hang the sack on the clothesline to dry. Mom was always thrilled when she got a print suitable for making pajamas, aprons, or skirts for her little girls.

Bringing home a newborn, plus having a toddler and my three-year-old brother named Joe running around proved to be a bit much for my poor mother and she soon succumbed to a nervous breakdown. So, when I was six weeks old, I was sent to stay with my Aunt Beanie and Uncle Bob Solomon until mother was well again.

Here I am at about one year old

Mother told me that when they went to bring me home again, Aunt Beanie had become quite attached and didn't want to give me back. Up until the day my Aunt Beanie died she always treated me like a second daughter, and her own daughter, Kaye, always referred to me as "Lil Sis." I always looked up to her. She was eight years older than I. She was a majorette at Otterbein High School. Several years later I became a majorette at my high school and Kaye gave me several uniforms and her baton.

Back in the 1940's there were no seat belts in cars and no car seats for infants and toddlers. We would literally either lay or stand on the seat while traveling down the road. When I was three years old, my mother was coming home from Ross and Verdie Smith's filling station a mile from our house. I fell against the door handle and tumbled out onto the gravel road. In a panicked state, my mother looked in the rearview mirror and saw me lying in the middle of the road, crying but miraculously uninjured except for a few minor scrapes and bruises. It was hard to convince my brother of that, however. Up until the day he died, Joe always said I was "messed up in the head" from that fall! My brother was three and a half years older than I and always found great pleasure in teasing me. At a young age, he decided to give his sisters nicknames. He always referred to Linda as "Sis" and called me "Tootsie," later shortening it to "Tudie." All through school these became household names and I don't remember him ever calling us by our given names again.

There were no kindergartens back in the 1940's. I began first grade when I was only five years old, very immature and scared beyond belief. My mother wanted her twins to go through school together so I was forced to attend at a very young age. The first six weeks were a disaster. Odie Reese was our bus driver. I would cry when mother put me on the bus. Then I cried every day at school for several weeks. One day my teacher, Mrs. Sewell, took me out into the cloakroom and spanked me and told me to grow up! I never liked that teacher and today I can still see her face vividly when I recall that horrible first year of school.

The school back then was a large brick building that housed all 12 grades. We even ate lunch with the high school age students. We also shared the same library and gym. There was a lot of interaction with all the grade levels. Whenever there was an assembly hall or pep session for our basketball team we all got to attend. It was held during the last period of the day in the gymnasium.

There were 12 schools in Tippecanoe County. We were all great rivals and when the drawings were held for basketball tourneys, competition kicked in with full force. Basketball was by far the most popular sport in school. Our schools were so small that there were not enough boys in high school to form football teams.

The county, sectional, and regional basketball tourneys were always played at Jefferson High School on 9th Street near downtown Lafayette.

Unlike today, all of the students took great pride in their teams. We had student blocks to cheer on the teams, led by meticulous cheerleaders. The student body sat together, all dressed alike, sporting white gloves, and many times forming impressive words and formations from large cards that the block would hold up on cue. At the end of the tourney, an award would be given to the school with the most spirit and pride. This award was as cherished as winning the basketball tourney itself.

The county tourney was always one of the highlights of our school year. The boys would play in the semi-finals on Saturday afternoon. If they made it to the final game on Saturday night, we always got permission to walk downtown between games. We would go to a movie or the McCord's Candy Shop on 6th Street with our friends, chanting school cheers all the way. This made us feel especially loyal to our school!

About two years after I graduated from Montmorenci with 17 students in my class, they consolidated with Otterbein to form Benton Central High School.

Chapter 3

The Singing Booher Sisters

A MAJOR PART OF MY CHILDHOOD was spent on music and singing publicly. Looking back, I realize how much time my mother devoted to introducing us to a lifetime of appreciation for music.

During this same time period, my dad was teaching Joe the art of farming. Joe was always out in the field with dad, and during the winter months they would be out in the tool shed building go-karts and model airplanes together. Joe never participated in sports. He would come home after school, hop on a tractor and work in the fields until dark. Since our farm has been in the family for six generations, I'm convinced that all Booher men are born to farm!

When Linda and I were five years old our mother began teaching us Sunday school songs. Dad had a natural ear for music and became our critic. Within a short time they discovered that their little girls had the ability to carry a tune, and I also had the gift to harmonize. By the time we entered elementary school, we were entertaining publicly at churches and talent shows. As the years progressed, we sang at county and state fairs, weddings, funerals, festivals, and TV and radio shows.

At ten years of age, we sang on the Morris B. Sach's Amateur Hour in Chicago and won an engraved watch that I still have today. During the teen years, we had a weekly Sunday morning radio broadcast on WASK. Our dad gave a short sermon, we girls sang a few songs and mother played the piano. This was a part of our lifestyle for several years. Every Sunday morning mother would wake us at 7 a.m. and we would suck on lemons all the way to the radio station on McCarty Lane in Lafayette. It was a live broadcast so there was no room for errors. The air time was supported by listeners who would send in money. Apparently we didn't have a very large fan club as the program folded after four years!

Linda and I [L] singing with the Curly Meyer's Band at Shady Acres, Mulberry, IN, 1953

Our parents opened a savings account for Linda and me as we began winning money in talent shows. By the time we graduated from high school we had saved nearly $2,000. Fifty years ago, that was a lot of money!

One night a week, mother would pick us up after school and take us to Mahara's Music Center for piano lessons. Later I also took accordion lessons and played in an accordion band. We also took voice lessons from a very strict teacher named Elizabeth Sharpless. She would begin our session with boring musical scale exercises and then progress into some songs with simple choreography. She was the director of the Children's Summer Theatre on Memorial Island in Columbian Park. During the summer months, Linda and I were beckoned to sing in their outdoor amphitheatre. The mosquitoes were horrible! If we performed well, mom and dad would treat us to a frozen custard on the way home.

Mother spent many hours making costumes and evening gowns for us to wear while entertaining. I don't know if my sister had a sex change or what, but I do remember that around the age of ten, she was always dressed like a boy whenever we were on stage! Of course I was the adorable little girl. Mother always had props for us to use and rigged up this stand that held a little brown jug. We then sang "A Penny A Kiss." We sang that number for years, many times at the request of our so-called "fan club!" We recorded several songs on the old 78 rpm records and, when Linda turned 65, I converted all the songs to CD and surprised her. The quality of the recording was bad but the memories were unequaled!

Mother kept a scrapbook that held articles whenever our name or picture appeared in the Journal and Courier newspaper. She would proudly paste the news clips in the book. I still have the little brown jug sitting on my dresser at home but, to this day, I wonder whatever happened to that treasured scrapbook.

Linda [R] and I [L], April 5, 1953

Chapter 4

Don't Fence Me In

YOU CAN TAKE THE GIRL OUT of the country but you can't take the country out of the girl! I love the wide-open spaces. Growing up on the farm has probably brought the most cherished memories of my lifetime. My mother and father were not only wonderful parents, but also devoted teachers. They taught us all we needed to know to become responsible, independent adults.

Even though I felt it was not in my best interest at the time to learn to cook and sew, our mother enrolled us in 4-H at the age of ten. She taught us the responsibility of starting a project and following through to the end.

We were required to try around 20 recipes and bake them for our family. We were required to keep a record book and jot down comments on our finished product. Dad loved cookies, as well as all sweets, so he was our designated critic. Being the kind and gentle man that he was, he would avoid negative comments by saying, "Well, it really wasn't my favorite," or "That was okie-dokey!"

Sewing was definitely not one of my highly regarded projects. I can remember sitting at the sewing machine in the corner of our dining room. Tears of frustration would be rolling down my cheeks as I wanted to be outside riding my horse. Mother would be sitting close by and she would say, "I'll rip out the seam for you if you'll just try to sew it again." She would console me by saying, "I know you can sew a straight line. I've seen you do it before."

Mom stuck by my side all summer until it was time for the county fair and sure enough, whether it be baking, clothing, crafts, or gardening, we always brought home a blue ribbon. We also exhibited chickens and cattle at the Tippecanoe County Fair but we never excelled in animal judging.

Thank you always, Mom, for teaching me to sew. As I became a mother, and now a grandmother, sewing has become a favorite hobby of mine. I can make my own curtains, clothing, and craft projects for friends and family. Many of my girlfriends ask me to alter their clothes or sew craft projects for them. They are very envious and always comment, "I wish my mother had taught me to sew."

As a tribute to my mother and father after they passed away I recycled a lot of their clothes and made teddy bears for all ten of the great-grandchildren from my dad's flannel shirts. Then I made a quilt from my mother's clothes. The quilt pieces are in the design of a sprinkling can, surrounded by flowers, with centers from the buttons of her clothes. The pattern reminds me of her love for flowers. Every summer their farm was a showplace. Mom and dad took great pride in their home. The place always looked immaculate both inside and out.

The quilt I made from Mother's clothes and two teddy bears made from Dad's old clothes. I finally finished the quilt in 2012, 10 years after she passed away.

Dad was as particular about his fields as mother was about her house! You knew what day of the week it was by the chores she was performing. Boy, did she ever have a meticulous schedule! Monday was washday. She had an old wringer washing machine in the basement and always hung the clothes outside to dry. She would spend all day Tuesday standing in the kitchen beside an ironing board. Friday would be spent running errands in town. Saturday was cleaning day and we were responsible for tidying our own rooms. Linda and I were required to take turns baking a dessert for the weekend. The finished product would give us credit towards our 4-H project. Sunday was devoted to the Lord. Sunday school and church were not optional. They were mandatory. We were taught to be thankful for all that we had. All of our meals began with a prayer. We three children would take turns reciting it.

"I thank thee Heavenly Father for the home I love so well
For Mother and for Father, for more than I can tell
For food I eat, for clothes I wear, for dear friends everywhere
I thank thee Heavenly Father. Amen."

Montmorenci Methodist Church

Gathering eggs was one of my favorite chores on the farm. It was like going on a treasure hunt! You always knew when a fresh egg had been laid by the proud clucking of the hen.

Every spring, Mother would order 400 baby chicks from Kissell's Egg Hatchery in Lafayette. I would love to just sit out in the brooder house and listen to the peeping of the three-day-old baby chickens. They were adorable little yellow fuzz balls! It was our job to help Mom pour egg mash in these long skinny feeders that had three long paddles going down the middle. I never did figure out what those long blades were for except to send the baby chicks catapulting whenever one landed on the spinning wheel! We had to place water stations very carefully amid the ground corncobs on the floor so as not to spill the water. Damp corncobs could easily cause a baby chick to get chilled and die. We would fill quart jars with water and turn them upside down into a tin saucer, and out bubbled the water!

Delivery day was always exciting for Mother. Perhaps it was because this was her very own special income from the farm. She also sold eggs to Kissell's. They would bring a truck to our farm once a week and pick up the eggs that we had gathered and graded. She had these indented shallow boxes in the basement. She would hold each egg up to a light before placing it in the box to be sure it was fresh. A cloudy egg was old and an egg with a harmless red fleck in the yolk was distasteful to city folk. A white bullseye on the yolk was a fertilized egg.

Mother needed to buy chicks each year because we would sell some of them as fryers, foxes would sometimes get into the henhouse, and some of those chicks would provide us great Sunday dinners. Yes, we often had mean roosters in the chicken lot! We had to pass through the chicken lot to get to our garden. We kept a long stick at the gate to be used as a weapon in case one of the roosters decided to spur us. If one was successful, Mom would single him out, grab the hatchet, and we would have homemade chicken and noodles the following Sunday!

Perhaps the most vivid memory I have of raising chickens on the farm occurred one day after mother had just bought a flock of baby chicks. They arrived in the spring while the nights were still quite cold. Infrared lights were needed to keep the chicks warm. It was very tricky placing the lights at just the right height. Placing them too low could catch the corncobs on fire and placing them too high could cause the chicks to chill. One morning mother left the farm and forgot to turn off the heaters in the brooder house. It got quite warm that day and, when we returned at dusk and opened the brooder house door, the smell of burning feathers came drifting through the air! Over 100 baby chicks had suffocated. I can remember trying to revive some of the dying chicks by manually dipping their little beaks in water. Mother was in tears. It is amazing how some of these events remain clearly in your head for decades!

The farm where I grew up, 5609 West 1000 North, West Lafayette, Indiana.

Dad was a near chain-smoker in his early middle age and smoked nearly two packs of Raleigh cigarettes a day! Mother would save the coupons attached to the cartons and then redeem them for kitchen appliances, toasters, coffee pots, etc. that were in the Raleigh Redemption Catalog. Nearly every morning I would awaken to my dad hanging over the back fence, hacking and coughing. He gave up cigarettes when he was 50 years old, however, when he got pneumonia at 91 years of age, the doctor said he could tell by looking at Dad's x-rays that he had been a heavy smoker in his younger years as his lungs were just black!

Dad worked many long nights in the field but during the winter months I can still see him sitting in his green overstuffed chair with matching footstool, just snoring away. Beside him would be The Prairie Farmer, Popular Mechanics, Successful Farming, and Life magazines. Dad loved to read and was a wealth of knowledge to all who knew him. No matter the age or gender of the person, he could always strike up a conversation.

Dad: "… in his green overstuffed chair with matching footstool, just snoring away."

Dad would arise early in the morning and during the winter months we would hear him down in the basement stoking the furnace. We had a coal chute extending to the outside and a large coal bin and corncob bin in the basement. When coal was delivered it would make a loud banging sound as it went sliding down the chute from the truck to the basement. The coal and cobs would fuel our furnace all winter. I guess we were recycling even back in those days, as these were the leftover cobs from corn shelling.

Winters on the farm seemed more brutal than they are today. Perhaps it was because we lived out in the country where the fields all had fences to catch the snow and let it pile up. The wind would come howling at night like a freight train and literally shake our windows and make little snowdrifts on the interior windowsills of our upstairs windows.

Our upstairs bedrooms were quite cold and it took all the stamina we could find to crawl out from under the covers on those blustery winter mornings.

If we caught cold, mother would heat camphorated oil on the stove in an old Mason jar lid, dip a cotton ball in that stinky oil, and rub it all over our chest. Then she would layer us with an old undershirt of Dad's and then our PJ's and send us off to bed with a vaporizer running full blast with Vick's VapoRub floating through the air. If that wasn't enough to cure us, Miss

Alenduff was called the next morning to schedule target practice with Dr. Jones! He gave us a shot of penicillin in our buttocks that was so painful we could hardly walk for two days!

Snowstorm at the Farm

On a couple of occasions, when we were really ill, the doctor actually came out to our farm and made a house call. This is unheard-of today.
On winter school mornings, Dad would stand at the window and alert us when the school bus was coming down the road. We have pictures of the snow piled so high on the road leading to our house that it looks like the bus is coming through a tunnel!

Many of our winter evenings after school were spent sledding and ice-skating on Sydney Farney's farm pond alongside the old road east of our house. There was not enough field tile back in those days to drain off all the excess water, and ponds would freeze over and create a great recreation area for the country kids.

I remember the blizzard of 1978. The snow was so deep that we could stand on top of a snowdrift and walk out onto our roof! Everything was at a standstill. The motels were all full; Interstate 65 was closed, so the media was asking local residents to open up their homes to stranded motorists along the way. Thank goodness the winters seem to have gotten milder over the past several years.

Snowstorm March 1960

Then came summer on the farm; this was a busy time, preparing for the long winter ahead. Mother had a huge garden as well as several rows of sweet corn out in the field. She also had cherry and apple trees and rhubarb. Every summer she would can over 300 quarts of produce. I can still visualize all the mason jars lined up like soldiers down on the basement shelf behind this curtain she had made out of chicken mash feed bags.

Grandma Booher would come out to the farm with her bib apron on, and sit under a shade tree in the backyard and shell garden peas or snap green beans all afternoon. Meanwhile Mother would be slaving in the kitchen beside a hot stove and a boiler full of canning jars. They would process these vegetables all afternoon. The next morning Mother would check the seals on the jars and proudly carry each one to the basement for storage.

All of the corn would be brought out of the field in a wagon with the kernels still attached to the ear. Very few farmers owned a corn sheller so you would have to wait your turn until one was available to come to your farm. This was always a busy day for the neighborhood farm wives. They would get together and cook a huge meal at noon for all the men as a thank you for all their hard work while shelling corn. Nowadays, all this is done in the combine. I can still taste those delicious homemade pies served with those festive noon meals!

"Neither snow nor rain" . . . the mail still comes . . .

If a farmer in the area became ill or injured, all the neighboring farmers would choose a day to bring their equipment to the ailing farmer's fields and harvest his entire crop in a day. One of our neighbors got his arm caught in the corn picker, requiring the amputation of his arm. By the time he was released from the hospital, all of his grain was in the corncrib.

One of the reasons I miss the farm life is because of the close relationship among farm families. They seem to look after each other and all settle close by, generation after generation. It is a bond that is unequaled. I wish I could go back.

Chapter 5

The Good Ol' Days

TELEVISIONS WERE MAKING their debut in the home so, if we got our homework finished before 8 P.M. on Monday nights, we were allowed to stay up an extra 30 minutes and watch "I Love Lucy." Unlike today, there was no daytime television and broadcasting ended and stations went off the air at midnight.

Dad's favorite TV shows were Red Skelton, Lawrence Welk, Ed Sullivan, and The Dean Martin Variety Show. We had few programs to choose from. Those wealthy enough to have an antenna attached to the roof of their home were able to pull in three channels by way of a "roto-rooter" box inside the home that would remotely rotate the antenna.

Sunday night was always popcorn night, compliments of dad. He thought no one knew how to make popcorn quite as perfectly as he did! He had a favorite heavy-duty pan and would place one kernel of corn in lard and, when it popped; he would add the rest and then shake the pan vigorously until the last kernel popped. As a special treat, he would sometimes melt butter on the stove and then pour it over the popcorn. That was a delicacy unequaled! Now, in the days of the microwave oven, I doubt that our grandkids have ever seen popcorn made quite that way. If we were out of the store-bought kernels it was never a problem. Dad would go down in the basement storeroom and grab several dried ears of popcorn hanging from a nail that he had brought in from the field. Dad would strip the kernels from the cob and then proceed with his delicacy.

Today's teens could not survive without cell phones and texting their friends. We had never heard of such devices. We had an old crank-type box phone hanging on the dining room wall, much like the one you saw on the old "Andy Griffith Show." We would manually ring up the operator by cranking the handle on the side of the box. We would tell her the number of the party we were trying to reach and she would connect us. Then we would speak into a megaphone-shaped tube and hold another piece, called a receiver, up to our ear. There would be as many as 17 people on our party line and many old ladies in the neighborhood would "listen in" to get all the latest gossip. We would need to listen for our own ring as several would sound into your home. I remember ours as being a long-short-long. We modernized over the years and were assigned our first private number, which was 23210. Eventually it was changed to 302F2. It seems rather freaky that I can remember our telephone numbers from over 50 years ago and can't even remember what I had this morning for breakfast!

Mother would go to the phone and crank one long ring to get the operator. Then she would say "43 please" and be connected with my Aunt Beanie in Otterbein. My Grandma Solomon lived in Otterbein for 87 years and never had a car or telephone. Whenever we needed to contact her, we would call Aunt Beanie and she would relay the message.

Dad would come in from the tool shed at lunchtime after working on a broken piece of farm machinery and call International Harvester to get a replacement. He would say "Hello, parts?" and Linda and I would literally roll on the floor in laughter!

I can also remember my dad coming in at lunchtime and turning on the old Silvertone Radio that sat on our kitchen table. We would be required to remain very quiet as he leaned his ear towards that box to get the daily grain market report.

I feel that we've come farther with the telephone than any other household device. Today there are phones in nearly every room, and cell phones in the hands of nearly every adult and teen in the country. You can shop, and at the same time, talk to nearly anyone in the world. Your phone can text friends, send pictures, calculate your finances, keep your calendar, and wake you every morning with the alarm sound of your choice! Amazing that when I was a child, we had never dreamed of cell phones or computers and today they are considered necessities in every home.

One highlight of our summer was when our cousins, Diane and Karen Lucas, would come to visit us. They were city girls from Chicago so they found great enjoyment in hanging out on the farm.

Alongside our garage, we had a row of Bridal's Wreath bushes that were always in full bloom when our cousins were staying at our house. As entertainment for all of us, we would always stage a fake wedding and make beautiful brides' and bridesmaid's bouquets with those flowers.

Cousins on the farm circa 1949-1950. Front row: Jimmy and Judy
2nd row: Joe, Karen, Linda, Marcia, Phil (on trike), Me
Back row: Diane

My dad would also keep the cousins busy by hiring all of us to cut Jimson and Button weeds out of the bean fields. He would take us out to the field on a hot summer day and assign each of us a row. He would then carefully hand each of us a handle with a triangle shaped cutter on the end that he had made. At the end of the day, he would pay us three cents for each row we had cleaned. Apparently child labor laws had not yet come into effect!

Then during our early teen years we began to get bored during the summer. We were beyond toys and not ready for boys. Living in the country limited our social activities, so several of the girls on our country block decided to form a club. This "elite group" consisted of Carol Keller, Judy Lachmund, Marcia Booher, and Linda and me. We all rode on the same school bus so many of our early planning meetings were held on the bus before summer break began. Our mothers agreed that we could take turns biking to each other's homes as long as we called when we arrived to let them know we were safe. Through some very serious planning and secret ballot voting, we decided to call our group "The Busy Bicycler's Club." The hosting home was responsible for serving cookies and Kool-Aid. Dues were set at five cents.

I really don't remember how many summers our club was active but apparently it left a lasting impression. Now, over 50 years later, whenever the cousins get together in Florida we still laugh about our Busy Bicycler's Club!

Chapter 6

My Awesome Aunties

My grandfather, Joseph Booher, had two sisters who never married, Carrie and Katherine. They lived on the old homestead all of their lives. One of their brothers, Frank, married a lovely lady named Grace and she lived with them also. After Uncle Frank passed away, the three ladies remained there together. We always referred to them as the "Old Maids," however they were not nearly as old as the house where they lived. We children always considered it close to being haunted. Since these aunts had no children, they dearly loved to have us come for a visit. They had an awesome barn with a horse and buggy, but no electricity or running water in the home. I can still vividly picture the entire layout of their farmhouse, including the furnishings! They had a huge claw-foot oblong dining room table covered with a white crocheted tablecloth that they had made. There were kerosene lanterns throughout the home. The kitchen had an old wooden planked floor with a cast iron stove that produced the best tasting caramel corn that you've ever eaten.

If you wanted a drink of water, you would go into the milk shed, attached to the kitchen, and dip a blue enamel ladle down into the well and bring up a fresh drink of water. The children were always thirsty as this was such a novel way to quench our thirst in this manner.

Occasionally we would spend the night with our aunties. Evening entertainment consisted of listening to the old Victrola and cutting chains of paper dolls out of butcher block paper.

Heaven forbid if we needed to use the bathroom during the night. We would be told the night before to awaken one of our aunties. They would then take us outdoors and, with a lantern, lead us down a pathway to the outhouse. It was a very eerie walk and we would lay in bed until we almost wet ourselves before beckoning them to come to our rescue.

Frank Booher Homestead

Back in the 1950's it was commonplace, when a family member died, to hold the viewing in the home. Therefore, when Uncle Frank passed away, the body was brought back to the farm, and the coffin was placed in the front parlor. We were very young children at the time and the mere smell of the funeral flowers and the dead body in the home made it difficult for me to sleep there after his passing. For years after his death, I would peer through the cracks in the parlor door and swear he was still in there!

My dad's sister, Mildred, affectionately called Aunt Mid, also had no children. She loved kids however and taught first grade for over 40 years. She would invite all her nieces to her home every summer for a week of fun-filled activities. We would love to hang out in her milk shed and play old 78rpm records on her Victrola. She would spoil us with homemade cookies and take us on picnics to Butterfield Park where we would swim all afternoon and then come back to an outdoor picnic on the lake. Even though their farmhouse was across the road from Lake Shafer, Uncle Asher and Aunt Mid owned lake frontage across the road with a public picnic area along the water. Whenever Uncle Asher saw a car stop on his property, he would quickly run across the road and collect 50 cents for the use of his picnic tables.

Aunt Carrie (L) and Aunt Kate

Aunt Mid's & Uncle Asher's farmhouse, across from Lake Shafer

In the evening, Aunt Mid and Uncle Asher would take us to Ideal Beach, an amusement park on Lake Shafer. We loved going on the rides. This same amusement park is still operating at this same location in Monticello today, however the name has been changed to Indiana Beach.

Aunt Mid was a very dedicated aunt who never forgot a birthday. She also printed a nice note on the greeting card. We always attributed her printing to the fact that she was a first grade teacher. During all the years that I knew her, I never saw her write anything in cursive.

Aunt Mid always had her camera handy. She was thrilled whenever we stopped by to see her and always had fresh muskmelon or watermelon to serve us. She was a great cook and made yummy cookies and yeast rolls. You never left her home hungry or without having your picture taken. Looking back through the albums, one can always recognize the ones Aunt Mid took, as there will be someone in the picture holding a sign with the date and the reason for the occasion! Those pictures still bring a smile to all of us.

Left to right: Linda, Aunt Mid, Me

When Aunt Mid passed away, she left all of her wealth to charity and to her nieces and nephews. Thank you Aunt Mid for the wonderful time you spent with us creating memories. We will be forever grateful. A happy childhood lasts a lifetime.

Update: it is now February 2012. I am on my way back to Myrtle Beach, SC, from Florida after visiting the only two remaining aunties in my family. My mother has passed away so these two women have stepped in to become my mentors. Much of the family history for this book was obtained from Aunt Dora. She is such a sweet little lady.

Aunt Dorothy, my dad's sister, is now 96 years old and still lives alone. When I visited her two years ago, she took me to a water aerobics class in her community pool. She insisted that I wear one of her bathing suits and accompany her, so I obliged! Aunt Dorothy is as smart as any broker on Wall Street. She reads the paper and watches the stock market daily. She is one sharp cookie and as cute as one too. Go girls! We're anxiously awaiting your centennial year birthday parties.

Further update, April 2012: While this book was in production, my dear Aunt Dorothy passed away in her sleep on April 15, 2012, at the age of 97. Aunt Dora passed away shortly thereafter in May of 2012.

Sadly they will not be in Florida anymore when the cousins gather each winter. They will always be fondly remembered and will remain in our hearts forever. Thanks for being the foundation of the family, ladies ... you will be missed.

Now that my aunts have both been laid to rest, my cousins and I have become the oldest surviving members of our family. It's kind of a scary thought, but a real wake-up call as to how fast our lives pass by. It's another reason why we need to live each new day to its fullest and spread knowledge and joy to everyone we meet along life's unpredictable pathway.

Chapter 7

Good Night for A Little While

Booher Farmhouse, January 1960

IT IS A COLD WINTRY DAY, January 19, 1960. Unbeknown to me, this day will come back to haunt me every day for the rest of my life.

I was a sophomore in high school and had been out of school all week with a Type A flu virus. Mother was the Tippecanoe County school nurse so she felt obligated to go to work that day. She made a bed for me on the green floral sofa in the living room so that I could watch the snow gently falling outside the window. She reassured me that she would come home and check on me as soon as school was dismissed. She sat a TV tray beside the sofa, with my favorite RC Cola, gave me a comic book, and kissed me good-bye.

To this day, I don't know where dad went that morning as he was usually in the house during the cold winter months, sitting at his desk in the dining room with tax papers strewn all over the floor!

During the course of the day, my fever began rising rapidly. I became weak, disoriented, and fell into a deep coma.

When my mother returned from work, she found me very ill and unresponsive and with a fever of 105 degrees. They rushed me to the hospital where I remained in a coma for over a month. During this time, the Lafayette doctors told my parents that there was nothing more they could do. The virus had spread to my brain and, if I recovered, I would probably be a vegetable the rest of my life.

My pediatrician, Dr. David Jones, told my folks about a neuropsychiatrist in Indianapolis, Dr. C. K. Hepburn, who might be able to help but it would be quite expensive to have him come up and take a look at me. Without hesitation mom said, "Get him on the phone."

The next day, Dr. Hepburn drove up from Indianapolis, confirmed that I had encephalitis, and changed my medications. Within 72 hours I turned the corner and began to come out of my unconscious state.

Private duty nurses were hired to care for me 24 hours a day. When I look back on this today, I see the unconditional love parents have for their child. My parents were willing to give up all they had to save me. My dad never believed in insurance, so I know that financially this sickness must have cost them thousands of dollars. Being the wonderful, caring parents they were, the subject was never brought up!

When I awoke from the coma, Barb Price, one of my private duty nurses, was there to welcome me back into the world. She was always my favorite nurse as her husband, Sam, was the basketball coach at our high school. My boyfriend, Dick Sturgeon, was the star player on the team. They told me that during these weeks of hospitalization, when each day could have been my last, Dick refused to go to school. He sat outside my hospital room for days, never giving up hope that someday I would come out of this dreaded stupor. As young as we were at age15, he knew that we had a lifetime together ahead of us and he was not going to let that go.

When I began to recover and was sent home to be in bed for the next several months, Dick's sister Carolyn would drive him out to the farm several nights a week after school, as he wasn't old enough to have a driver's license. Linda and Carolyn would sit for hours on the kitchen floor playing jacks while Dick would sit on the bed beside me, hold my hand, and tell me how important it was to take my medicine and get my rest as we had a big future ahead of us.

Right after I went into the hospital, and the grim prognosis was made known, prayer chains were started, and churches and friends from all over the county began sending cards of encouragement. Before I left the hospital, over 350 cards had been sent. Our name was very familiar as my dad was a big farmer and my sister and I had sung at many events throughout the community. My mother bought a scrapbook and, while recovering, I spent my hours pasting the cards in the book. I always looked forward to the mail delivery as it gave me something to do while bedfast.

I missed the entire second semester of my sophomore year recuperating from this dreaded disease. We made numerous trips to Indianapolis to see the doctor and I had so many EEG's (electroencephalograms) that my head felt like a pincushion. Dick would skip school many times when I had an appointment and would sit in the back seat of our car and hold my sore head all the way home.

The next few years were ones I'd like to forget. I had numerous seizures and violent, uncontrollable nerve attacks as my body was trying to readjust to the memory loss, partial paralysis of my right arm, and brain damage from the sickness.

The love of my family and boyfriend surrounded me and helped me through this horrible time.

When I returned to school, I was still very weak so I started back for two hours, then half days.

These teen years were very cruel to me. I had lost a lot of my hair due to the high fever and I can still remember bolting out of the classroom in tears one day when a student behind me blurted out, "Oh, look, Sandie has a big bald spot on her head!" Dick found the boy after class and nearly bashed his head in on the metal lockers that lined the hallway.

I don't know what I would have done without my sister. She and Dick were both in my class and she was determined that I was going to catch up and walk down the aisle at graduation with the class that I had been in for the past 12 years. Mom and dad hired a private tutor and Linda would help me with my homework. Her patience was unconditional. My memory was so bad, she would stay up half the night quizzing me for a test until I had all the answers right, then she would get up early the next morning so that we could review before school and I would have forgotten everything she'd taught me! This went on all through the rest of my high school days. My "A" average that I had before my illness now dropped to "B's" and "C's", but she accomplished her mission and I walked down the aisle and graduated with my class!

I will be forever grateful to Linda for she had faith in me.

Chapter 8

Fashions and Traditions

FASHIONS WOULD COME AND GO much like today. Bubble shoes, bobby socks, and mini skirts all made their debut. Pierced ears and body tattoos were unheard of unless you were in the military or recently discharged from prison!

Two standard pieces of clothing that adorned every high school girl's closet were a class sweater and a senior skirt. A lot of time and money was spent designing your senior yellow cords, or corduroy skirt. Some students would paint their own, but if you really wanted to make a statement, you would have it professionally done. Of course Linda and I chose the latter! Mine had a character of Dennis the Menace, cartoon characters of Donald Duck and Porky Pig and, of course, Dick's name running down the vertical pleat in the back. We would select a certain day of the week when all the seniors would wear their yellow cords. The freshman could wear green cords, sophomores red, juniors gray, but absolutely no one other than seniors dared be caught in those yellow cords!

Poodle skirts were a given in your closet wardrobe, as well as a bouffant net can-can slip that made your skirt stand nearly straight out! I can't believe my modest mother actually let us walk out the door dressed like that. When we sat down our skirts nearly hit us in the face!

Unlike today, when parents' nights and weekends are consumed with kids' practices and ballgames, our Sundays were spent visiting relatives after mandatory Sunday school and church. Our Sunday ritual would actually begin on Saturday. Mom would spend the entire morning washing our hair. We had no shower so she would make us lie down on the kitchen counter and hang our heads in the sink. We were usually treated to Tame Crème Rinse after shampooing. If she had none on hand, she would rinse our hair with rainwater she had collected from the downspouts. Supposedly this was to keep our hair soft.

Then the real torture began. Mom would wind our hair up in these hard pink plastic rollers that had these nearly barbed wire appendages sticking out of them! Then she would secure them by poking these plastic-looking toothpick skewers nearly all the way through our skulls! Mom tried to get her mission accomplished early in the day so that our hair could dry. There were no such things as blow dryers or curling irons and she always said she didn't want us to go to sleep with a wet head! However it was nearly impossible to sleep anyway with those hard rollers surrounding your head. It was like sleeping on a cactus!

I remember getting our first hair dryer when Linda and I were in high school. It was much like the commercial ones you see in beauty shops today, except of the portable variety. The dryer was a plastic dome-shaped suitcase with a hose inside that you would attach to a large plastic-looking "lampshade"! Linda and I each got one for Christmas and we were stylin'!

Then along came pantyhose. Wow! No more garter belts. We were teenagers when pantyhose made their debut. I think we spent more time putting them over our heads and disfiguring our faces at slumber parties than we did wearing them on our legs!

Class rings were a treasured piece of jewelry. A salesman would come to our high school and present all the styles he had to offer. This was always an exciting time for dating couples, as they would exchange rings as soon as they arrived. Of course the guys' rings were much too large to fit the girls' fingers so we had to get creative. For a while tape made a statement. We would roll it around the band until we got a tight fit, and then take fingernail polish and paint the tape a funky color. Then we progressed to angora yarn. We would wrap it round and round the band until it looked like we'd just shot a rabbit! We would spend as much time at night wrapping our boyfriend's ring in a color to match our next day's attire as we would on our homework.

Mothers can always read your mind, so she told me I had to wear my own class ring for six weeks until I traded it off to Dick. Well, things didn't go exactly as she'd planned. Within a week, his was on my finger and mine was on a chain around his neck!

Dick and I, going to Junior Prom, 1961

Dick was putting up hay the following summer after taking possession of my new class ring with the beautiful pearl setting. All I can say is, if you have a metal detector, it might be worth your while to scan that hay field south of Montmorenci High School. You never know what you might find!

As for me, being the responsible girl that I am, Dick's class ring is still sitting in my jewelry box at home.

Family Photo Album

My grandmother and her sisters. Bottom row L to R: Allie Dilts Frazier, b 1894, Zella Dilts Cox, b 1877, Laura May Dilts Parker, b 1886. Top row L to R: Cora Dilts Solomon 1888, Sarah Martha Dilts Burdge

Ross Solomon

Cora Solomon

Joe and Carrie Booher

Grandma Solomon & my mom (Doris Isabel Booher)

Playing "house": Aunt Mid, born 5/24/1909, Aunt Dot (Dorothy), born 1-26-15, in the bed

L-R Joe and Carrie Booher, Aunt Carrie, Aunt Grace, Uncle Frank, Aunt Kate at the old homestead where Uncle Frank was brought back for viewing after his death

Mom (L) a cheerleader at Otterbein High School

My mother, Doris Isabel Booher

My grandparents Joe & Carrie Booher congratulating me on my high school graduation. It was a great accomplishment after a long recovery in high school from encephalitis.

Florida 2008 -- Front row: Aunt Dorothy, Aunt Dora
Back row: Diane, Karen, Phil, Marcia, Me, Judy

My visit to the farm in 2006. Modern tractors help get the job done now.

L-R: Karen, Phil, Nancy, Ray, Marcia

A.J. Booher, grandson who has taken over farming our land. He is the 6th generation of the family to carry on the tradition.

Dick and I at Myrtle Beach, and at our last Christmas together

Chapter 9

I'm Gonna Marry That Boy Someday!

ONE OF THE HIGHLIGHTS OF MY fifth grade year, besides finding the boy of my dreams, was the fact that I won the fifth grade spelling bee and moved on to represent our school in the Tippecanoe County Spelling Bee Contest. I was defeated after several rounds, but came in fifth and felt very proud. I still have my certificate stowed away in my memory box. To this day I do not excel in science, math, or history, but boy, can I ever spell! I give credit for this ability to my second grade teacher Bernice (Moore) Moyars. She was an awesome phonics teacher and drilled us until we had it right. She was not going to let us proceed into the next grade level until we knew how to sound out words and spell correctly. It bothers me today to see so many misspelled words in the newspaper and on signs in front of businesses. Nowadays the kids don't need to know how to spell; the computer does the spell checking for them! Perhaps we need to get rid of the computer and get Mrs. Moyars back in the classroom.

In December of each year, a sixth-grade girl from each school in our county was selected to be a "Snow Princess" and ride on the float in the Lafayette Christmas Parade. I was chosen. Even though I had been sick all week with an upper respiratory infection, mom bundled me up and I rode in the parade, waving to the crowd along the way. I felt like I was "Queen for a Day!"

Approaching my junior year, I was selected to twirl my baton at the home basketball games. Along with three other girls, we would have a designated area to perform our routines on the gym floor. I made my uniforms for both my junior and senior years. I would stay after school one night a week and give baton lessons to six little girls in our elementary school. They each paid me fifty cents for a one-hour lesson. Back in those days the pay was good, but the payoff was even greater! You see, while I was giving baton lessons on the stage at one end of the gym, Dick was enduring basketball practice at the other end of the court. Lessons and practice both ended at 5 p.m. We always told our parents it was 5:30. That gave us extra time to be together one night a week. We lived in those forgotten years where parents were in control! No dating on school nights, and only two dates on weekends. Dick and I always went out on Saturday night so we had to choose between Friday night or Sunday afternoon for our second date. I lived at home until I married at age 21 and still had a curfew of 1 a.m. on weekends. A girl never drove her car and picked up a boy, and calling a boy on the phone was never allowed. That's why we had to get a little crafty at times!

One great memory of junior high and high school were the slumber parties that one of our classmates would host nearly every Friday night. We would bring an overnight bag to school and about six girls would board the hosting friend's school bus and giggle and laugh all the way home in preparation for a fun-filled weekend.

When I look back at some of the crazy shenanigans we pulled, it's a wonder that I'm here today to write about it! Of course, when you are a teenage girl you have one thing on your mind—boys! We would all pile into one car and take off into town, radio blasting, girls screaming, and, of course, no seatbelts! The levee in West Lafayette was nothing like the one you see today. An old Park N' Eat Drive In and a Big Wheel Restaurant were located side by side. You would pull your car up to a speaker, place your order and a girl would bring your food out on a tray and secure it to your half-opened window. Of course, we were way more interested in impressing boys than eating food, so we would cruise for hours, first around one restaurant and then around the other, just hoping to somehow be noticed by our Prince Charming.

If one of our girlfriends was having a spat with her boyfriend, we found great joy in driving by his house late at night with the headlights off, blasting the horn all the way. If this didn't get his attention, we would T.P. (toilet paper) his front yard until it looked like a winter wonderland! We ended up in the ditch more than once trying to make our getaway. Looking back, I feel that we were lucky that someone didn't get injured.

My sister and I did much double dating throughout high school. I especially remember how much fun we had while dating two guys who were best buddies, Eddie Marshall and Dick Sturgeon. These boys were inseparable. This brought an even closer bond between Linda and me as we would prepare to go out on our dates together.

In my baton-twirling outfit, 1961

Mother always had a curfew for us. If we would sit out in the driveway for too long after returning from our dates, she would begin flashing the outdoor garage light off and on as a warning to say goodnight and get in the house. Linda and I would get the message and come inside like the good girls our folks thought we were. We would run upstairs to our room. Then the boys would begin racing their car up and down the old road east of our farmhouse with the lights off on Dick's old '53 Chevy. Linda and I would shine a flashlight out of our bedroom window and blink it off and on as a code we had given the boys. When we gave them the "all clear" signal, they would come speeding back down the gravel road. Boy, the crazy things we did for love!

Dick and Eddie were great basketball players and loved to drive to the Indiana Beach Amusement Park in Monticello and win teddy bears for us. At one time, Linda and I had over 40 giant bears lining the shelves of the small upstairs bedroom that we shared.

My dog "Buttons" with the stuffed animals that Dick would win for me at Indiana Beach. Small upstairs bedroom that Linda and I shared.

Linda was always popular and beautiful, and dated several boys throughout high school. Not me. I knew in the fifth grade who I was going to marry. Mrs. Biery was our teacher. One day she announced that we had a new student joining our class from Pine Village, about 25 miles from West Lafayette; little Dickie Sturgeon. He was by far the smallest boy in the room.

That afternoon I went home from school with butterflies in my stomach and a joyful feeling I'd never felt before. That night, before going to sleep, I told my sister a little secret that was just between the two of us, "I'm gonna marry that boy someday."

From that day forward our love blossomed. Call it puppy love or call it chance, but Dick and I both knew when we were ten years old that someday we would marry! You will find out later in this book that we were right.

Of course we were too young to date but that didn't stop us from always choosing each other on our team at recess or passing little flirtatious notes from one desk to another.

Dick had no appreciation for music and had no sense of rhythm, so he found dancing quite awkward. We would just sit on the bleachers during sock hops and hold hands and talk about our future.

Dick's family was quite poor and my parents thought that their little girl could do better, but we were determined to prove them wrong and boy did we ever!

Dick's father was a hired hand on a small farm and lived in a small tenant house that was barely able to keep their family warm in the winter. His mother was an invalid with multiple sclerosis. To this day, I can still see Dick's dad, dressed in his old bib overalls, pushing his wife in a wheelchair into the gymnasium so that she could see their son play basketball. Dick was an awesome player and always gave a spectacular performance. Many nights he would score over 30 points a game! He was very small but a very quick point guard and deadly from the three-point range, although back then we only got two points, no matter the distance.

Dick worked hard through high school helping farmers put up hay, pumping gas at filling stations, and mowing yards. His family was on welfare so he supported himself almost totally all through high school. I had learned to sew through 4-H, so many times I would make the two of us matching shirts to wear to school. Those were the nicest clothes he had, and he was always so happy to get them. The two of us felt even more like a couple being dressed alike!

One secret which we never told our parents even up until the day they died was that Dick and I were secretly engaged since the age of 16! He saved up enough money from working on the farm to buy me a cheap diamond ring when we were juniors in high school. Dick proposed to me one night on a date and gave me the ring. From that night forward, I would put it on when I got in his car to go out on a date, and then carefully stow it away in the ring box and put it back in the glove compartment when we got home. This went on for over four years. When Dick asked my folks for their permission to marry me, I had to act very surprised and excited when he presented the engagement ring to me!

I must tell you that the ring was so cheap that all the sets had fallen out by the time we celebrated our tenth wedding anniversary. Dick took the band to a jeweler and had him melt it down into a dainty necklace. Then, on our 25th wedding anniversary, we bought matching wedding bands. This supports the fact that money doesn't buy happiness; the band was never as special to me as that old wedding ring with the empty prongs. It's the fond memories that last a lifetime.

At age 21, we were married in the Congress Street Methodist Church in Lafayette, Indiana. We had a beautiful evening Christmas wedding on December 11, 1965. It was followed by a cake and ice cream reception in the church basement. I dreamed of a beautiful snowy evening, but instead it was 40 degrees and raining cats and dogs! Our plan was to drive to the Terre Haute House the night of our wedding, and then spend two days at Santa Claus, Indiana. It rained so hard on the way to the hotel that we were both mentally and physically exhausted by the time we arrived. We were also starving, so we found ourselves running around at 2 a.m. looking for a place to eat. We finally found this old, 24-hour truck stop. I can still see the shocked look on the waitress' face when we told her it was our wedding night!

Introducing Mr & Mrs Richard Sturgeon, December 11, 1965

Chapter 10

Boy, Oh Boy, Oh Boy, Oh Boy!

I GRADUATED FROM MONTMORENCI High School in 1962, along with my sister, Linda, and boyfriend Dick Sturgeon. There were 17 students in our class. Only six were boys so the picking was slim. I lucked out and got a gem!

After high school, I enrolled in Union Hospital School of Nursing in Terre Haute, Indiana. After I studied there for one year they terminated their program and all the student nurses were required to transfer. I spent the following summer taking classes at Indiana State College and then moved back home to enroll in the Saint Elizabeth School of Nursing in Lafayette. After a year of study there I suffered a back injury, plus I was still struggling with memorization due to my prior brain illness. We were now doing clinicals in the hospital wards and I couldn't remember the procedures, and the administration of drugs was going to be a real problem. I decided to leave school. I hated myself for not fulfilling my lifetime dream of becoming a nurse. Both my mother and sister are registered nurses and I felt I let them down. To this day I regret never getting my degree.

While attending nurses' training at St. Elizabeth Hospital, I lost one of my best friends, Alice Hawkins, whom I had chummed around with since first grade. After graduation, she had gone on to become an airline stewardess. While I was driving home from class one day, a news bulletin came over the radio that a Purdue plane had crashed while en route to pick up the team, killing both the pilot and the airline stewardess. I was driving my dad's farm pick-up truck and the radio wasn't too clear. But even though they mispronounced her name, I knew it had to be Alice. The road home, down old highway 53, seemed to take forever. I was crying and shaking uncontrollably by the time I pulled into the driveway at the farm. Mother was waiting at the back door. I looked at her and said, "It was Alice, wasn't it?" She said nothing but I knew, by the way she held me in her arms, my best friend would now be just a memory.

I began working at Purdue University in 1964 and continued my job as a receptionist after marriage until I became pregnant with my first child.

We lived in the upstairs of this old maid's house. It was located in Otterbein. The landlady's name was Viola Mann. It was our first home. We were honeymooners and thought we owned a castle! The rent was $35.00 per month. After a year, she raised it to $40.00 per month and we almost moved out due to the added expense.

We shared the same entryway as Miss Mann so she would stick her head out into the hallway every time we would come and go, just to check on us.

We bought a rickety old bed at a yard sale and every night the slats would go crashing to the floor! She would stick her head out the window and holler, "Is everything okay up there?"

We would laugh hysterically. Since she was an old maid, she probably never realized why those boards just wouldn't stay in the frame.

Our firstborn son, Steven Wayne, was born on October 2, 1968, while we were living in this apartment. When he became mobile, we were afraid he might fall down the stairs, and carrying the stroller up and down the stairway every time we went for an outing became a hassle.

We rented a three-bedroom ranch home on the next street for $75.00 per month. There was a big fenced backyard with apple trees and a sandbox. To us it was a plantation! I can still picture Steve, crying and kicking, as we would pick him up out of his sandbox each evening and bring him in to get ready for bed. A typical boy, he loved getting dirty!

Dick had been working at National Homes when we got married, but was now employed at Rea Magnet Wire in Lafayette. He worked the second shift so he bought a huge grain truck and hauled loads to Chicago as a second income. Steve loved riding in the "big truck" with daddy. Steve has now revealed to me that he was introduced to his first cigar in that big old grain truck!

Within two years another son was on the way. Scott Dwayne was born on December 12, 1970. Shortly thereafter, we bought a 20-acre farm with seven outbuildings, three miles west of the old West Point School on Turner Road.

Our first home with seven outbuildings on Turner Road, West Point, Indiana

Dick had now taken a job with Eli Lilly. This was a huge bonus for us. All of our children received free medications and their retirement plan was super. This was a much sought-after job and he felt fortunate to be hired. To this day, Eli Lilly has taken care of my prescriptions and medical needs. I also receive a widow's pension so I feel blessed.

Life on our mini-farm was a lot of fun, but it was exhausting. Dick would bring feeder calves home from the auction barn and we would feed them out, butcher them, and fill our freezer for the winter. One day Dick surprised me by bringing home a pair of three-day-old twin orphaned Angus calves. Steve and Scott had befriended them at the auction barn and had already named them "Pete" and "Repete" before we unloaded them into the barn. The boys bottle fed them for weeks and they became family pets.

I also raised chickens and sold eggs to neighbors. I had a huge garden and canned in preparation for winter. During this time, I became pregnant again but lost the baby at two months gestation due to physical exhaustion.

We were blessed with a third son, Skip Robert, on July 8, 1972. Skip was an adorable, curly haired little boy who loved to carry baby chickens around in the front pocket of his bib overalls. He loved all the animals on the farm. By this time we had a dog, barn cats, sheep, sows and baby pigs, calves, and chickens.

Dick thought we had the perfect family with three boys, but I had always dreamed of raising a little girl. I convinced him that the chances of having four boys in a row were pretty slim. Well, guess what? On October 10, 1974, we formed our own basketball team, Dick and his four boys! The boys at home were thrilled when Dick returned from the hospital with the news of the arrival of Shane Richard. Steve spoke up and said, "Oh good. Does this mean we can still run around the house in our underwear?" I had forewarned the boys many times during my pregnancy that the streaking through the house would have to stop if a baby sister arrived.

What a blessing this fourth little boy turned out to be! First of all, he cooperated and was born on my father's birthday, October 10, 1974. All the remaining years of my dad's life we would have a double birthday party. Shane has a picture of the two of them on every birthday celebration until grandpa's death in 2004.

We both worked very hard on the farm. We were young and living out our dream. Dick had a hog set-up with the Lafayette Co-op Elevator. They would deliver 700 head of feeder pigs to our feeding floor. Dick would keep them in confinement and feed them until they became market size. He would then take them to the auction barn and split the profit 50-50 with the elevator that had been supplying and delivering the feed to our farm.

Steve and Scott loved getting dressed up in their bib overalls and riding to the auction barn on Thursdays in the big truck. This was the men's day out! Dick said he would light up a cigar and the boys would talk non-stop all the way. Looking back, I think they must have been high on something as the boys now admit that their dad always let them have a puff of that nasty cigar!

I always looked forward to those Thursday livestock auctions as we now had two more babies in the home: Skip, a toddler, and Shane, a newborn. This gave me a relaxing day at home. We now had four little boys, so my maternal chores were cut by 50 percent on Thursdays! Dick had a rule that the boys must be potty trained before he would take them for long hauls in the big truck. Perhaps that is why I had all four of the boys out of diapers by the time they reached 21 months!

L-R Steve, Scott, Shane, and Skip. Billiards in the basement

When Shane was about six months old we moved to a four-bedroom ranch home on State Road 225, about a mile west of Battle Ground.

For the first year, I was miserable. I missed the farm. I missed my animals. I wanted to go back. I would love to go back there today if there was a log home sitting where the farmhouse stood. That has always been my ultimate dream.

Shane was a delightful child. He was always cooperative and kept up with his brothers all through childhood.

There continued to be this inquisitive mind inside me that wondered what it would be like to have a little girl with pink frills and dolls strewn throughout the house. Therefore, in 1978, when Shane was about three and a half years old, we became foster parents hoping to care for a little girl. Most of the infants were boys! We eventually got the answer to our prayers—a six week old, very malnourished and unresponsive six-pound pink bundle was delivered to our door via a caseworker from the Tippecanoe County Welfare Department. When the little girl was placed in my arms, I looked at her and knew this was going to be her forever home. We were not going to let her get away. The boys quickly named her "Sissy" which stuck for two years. Then in September 1982, parental rights were terminated. We quickly stepped in, legally adopted her, and she became Rebecca Dawn Sturgeon.

We had so much fun welcoming this little girl into our family—all pink frills, nothing but beautiful dresses with matching bows for her hair. We would take her to ball games looking like she was a flower girl in a wedding. Well, you guessed it! Being reared in a family with four athletic brothers, Becky soon found herself living out of the back of our station wagon while enduring hundreds of baseball games. She shared a TV room of nothing but sports and was eventually molded from a precious little princess into a strong-willed, sports-loving team mom of today, who now has two sons and an adopted son of her own! Go Becky! You're a great success story and you've made your mama proud.

Our four boys and Becky spent most of their childhood growing up at 8701 Tenskwatawa Drive in Tippecanunck Estates, north of Battle Ground on Road 900 North. It was at that location that Dick and I went on to foster over 100 more children.

This was such a rewarding mission. It was a calling from God to suffer the little children to come unto me. The Lord saved my life when I was 15, and I wanted to give Him something back in return. What better way than to care for the little children that he sent to this earth who had no one to love, nurture, and care for them? However, if I had it to do over again, I would try harder to put my family first. Many Friday nights when my boys were in high school, I was forced to tune into the radio and listen to my sons playing a football game, as I was at home with a newborn foster baby. The mere mention by the announcer of my sons scoring a touchdown or making a key play would cause the tears to come flowing down my cheeks. I would pace the floor with both excitement and shame with every play, feeling guilty that I was not there in person to see their glory.

As my children grew older they would recall those times and tell me how I had let them down. Their dad remained their hero until the day he died. He never missed a ballgame and always took our kids and their dates out to eat after a game. He was the perfect father.

Becky, 1982 and 1985—our little tomboy

Chapter 11

We Always Had Room for One More

EVEN THOUGH I ALREADY mentioned foster parenting in this book, I felt that my babies were worthy of at least one chapter of their own. When I told Skip that I was writing a life book, he spoke up and said, "Gee mom, it must be a big one. I'd think our experiences as a foster family would take a book in itself!" Even though his logic was right, I've tried to condense a few fond memories into just one chapter.

As stated elsewhere in this book, one of the main reasons we wanted to get involved in foster care was to bring a little girl into our home to complete our family. Now that we had our own basketball team, we needed at least one cheerleader!

After fostering ten baby boys, our first girl, a three and a half year old, arrived. I was in town shopping at the time, so Dick was ecstatic when the caseworker brought her to our door. He thought it would be a great surprise for me (as I mention several times in this book, Dick was all about surprises). When I came walking in the door with groceries in hand, Lori looked up at me and said, "You're not my real mom and I don't have to do anything you say!" Boy that must have been rehearsed several times with her natural mother before Child Protective Services intervened and took her away!

Lori stayed with us for three months. She was adorable and we loved her dearly, but she was as stubborn as a mule! When she left I told Dick, "If all girls are like this, I'm not sure I even want one!"

Scott seemed to always be the ingenious one and would come up with nicknames for the babies. Sometimes we were never given the actual name of the child. A few newborns came into the world with no name as the mothers had decided prior to delivery to release their babies for adoption. I always had high regard for this type of mother. They wanted a better life for their children and were not selfish enough to make them suffer. I felt this was the best way they could show their babies they loved them. If a mother is out on the street and knows nothing but a life of poverty, chances are the child will grow up to be the same way. That cycle must be broken.

We once fostered a ten-pound newborn baby boy that Scott named "Moose." We had an adorable Indian infant that was quickly tagged "Tyrone." Another unnamed baby boy arrived whom we lovingly named "Skeeter." This little guy lucked out and found a permanent adoptive home by the time he was ten days old. His name was quickly deleted and changed to Christopher by his new forever family.

Skip loved babies and spent a lot of time babysitting in our neighborhood. By the age of 11, he spent one entire summer watching three young pre-school aged brothers while their mother worked. Skip was very reliable; I don't think he missed a day of work all summer long. He was always in demand as a sitter because he loved kids and they loved him.

Skip and Amy were dating during our fostering years and would spend many nights just playing with the babies at the house! They became very attached to one little guy named Stevie. He was a very fast crawler and the boys encouraged him to move quickly by chanting, "Come on ugly Stevie!" Even though it sounded cruel, they meant it in a loving way. We entered him in the "Huggies Diaper Derby" in Lafayette, a race for crawling-aged babies only, sponsored by Huggies and Coca-Cola. One coach per entrant was allowed, but you could not touch the baby during the race, verbal commands only were allowed. Skip was our designated coach. He stood along the sidelines hollering, "Come on, ugly Stevie!" Even though the fans in the crowd were giving us a disgusted look, Stevie blew everyone away and we proudly came home with a year's supply of Huggies diapers and a year's supply of Coca-Cola products. It took a pick-up truck to haul everything home. We were thrilled and our baby did us proud.

One baby boy came into our lives and touched our hearts forever. His name was Gary. After about a year, his newborn sister, Rachel, joined him in our home. In the meantime, their mother became pregnant for a third time. The Welfare Department was to intervene as soon as the baby girl was born. Unfortunately, as with many cases of child abuse, the department is too overloaded to investigate every situation that is reported. The mother had schizophrenia and killed the baby before she could be placed in foster care.

After two and a half years, Gary and Rachel were released to a wonderful adoptive home. Even though we were allowed to help with the selection of their new parents, this was a very hard move for us. During our 39 years of marriage, this was one of the very few times I saw Dick cry. As the adoptive family drove away in their car, Dick wrapped his arms around our walnut tree in the front yard and cried like a baby for nearly an hour.

We often wondered why we punished ourselves like this. But our love for children ran so deep that we were willing to sacrifice pain in order to start a new life for a child. Many times we would pack up our family after a departure such as this and go away for a few days and stay in a hotel. It was just too hard to go back in and clean up the nursery until our hearts had healed.

Becky was like a little mother by the time she was five years old. She could diaper and feed a baby as well as I did. The caseworkers all marveled at her parenting skills. By the time she reached high school age, if I wasn't at home when we got the call from the Welfare Department, they would bring the baby out to Becky and she would have the bassinet moved into her room by the time I returned home!

The stories of these abused and neglected children go on and on. Many of them are too pathetic even to print. We once received a sibling group of five small children. It was a busy day for the welfare department. This family had 15 children. One of the daughters had been impregnated by her father, and they were all living out of a car!

We also fostered a pair of identical twin boys named Jimmy and Johnny for nine months. Their mother was only 12 years old and in the eighth grade when she became pregnant. We would keep the twins during the week while she attended junior high school and then take them back to her on the weekends. Even though she loved them and tried hard to care for them, she had no family support, and wasn't old enough to get a job. She released them for adoption before their first birthday.

We had our own melting pot around the dinner table on any given night of the week. We fostered bi-racial, Indian, Nigerian, Mexican, Negro, and Caucasian children. One cute Nigerian toddler was found roaming around the Purdue Campus at 3 a.m. when we got the call to go the police station and pick him up.

A special newborn, whom we fondly called Duke, probably taught us more than any other foster child who came through our doors. I knew as soon as the caseworker placed him in my arms that something just didn't feel right. He was so stiff and not like the cuddly babies that had been placed in my arms so many times before.

I received permission from the caseworker to take him to a specialist. He was diagnosed with cerebral palsy before the age of six months. I took him to therapy three times a week. We continued to foster him for a year. He learned to drag-crawl all over the house. Even though he could not sit up or eat without assistance, Duke never complained and was always smiling. He taught us to appreciate all that we had and to stop complaining over minor things. It took so little to make him happy; he thought he had the world by a string!

Duke was released to an adoptive home that already had adopted an older son with cerebral palsy. His new name became Jacob and he was blessed.

Our last foster child was a six-week-old failure-to-thrive child who stayed for two and a half years. Our kids named her "Peanut." Even though she was frail and malnourished, she quickly responded to our love and attention, and soon became an adorable, healthy toddler. She was like Becky's little sister; they were together constantly. When Becky was elected to the Battle Ground Junior High Cheering Squad, I made an identical uniform for Peanut and she became the team mascot and never missed a game.

Peanut had two older brothers in another foster home. When parental rights were terminated, the judge ordered that all three children be placed together. Our oldest son, Steve, had a truck at the time so the two of us were elected to take Peanut to her permanent home. Over the course of two and a half years, she had accumulated a lot of baggage including a little coupe riding car that she dearly adored. That last ride to Lafayette was horrible. I was crying so hard that I should not have been driving.

Peanut was strapped in the backseat and I just kept telling her "I love you" all the way to town. Steve tried to remain strong but the detachment got to both of us. After we delivered Peanut to her adoptive home, we just stood at the curb and cried. We knew at that moment that we could never put ourselves through this again.

**Left -- Becky, Battle Ground Junior High Cheerleader
Right --Peanut, in her matching uniform**

Peanut and Becky

This became our last year of foster parenting. We were featured in the Lafayette Journal & Courier newspaper as having been foster parents longer than anyone else in Tippecanoe County.

Even though our hearts were broken, we would not have traded those years for anything. We had fostered over 100 children and had learned so much about sharing our love with others.

We had given so much of our time but the rewards we reaped were even greater. Without foster care, we would never have gotten our daughter, Becky. This in itself made it all worthwhile.

Gary, one of my foster angels, safe in my arms

By A Foster Mother

Poor little child, standing in my door today
I don't know the reason, but God sent you my way.
All the things you own are in a paper sack
And my job is to love you till they send you back.
I don't know where you came from
Or what you've been through
And no matter how bad it was
Your home was home to you.
You knew what to do there
And you knew what to expect.
Well, here you stand at my door
And wonder what happens next.
You have so much to learn here.
How we live each day
And I know you wonder
Why in the world we act this way.
You probably don't know why you behave the way you do
And if I were in your shoes I might act that way too.
How can you be happy when your life is out of control?
You're supposed to be a good child
And do the things you're told.
No one asks you what you want
Or how you really feel.
I suppose you even wonder if all of this is real.
You had no say where you were born
Or who your family would be.
And somehow through life's crooks and turns
You end up here with me.
I know you miss your family because they are your own.
And even if they aren't so great
They are the only ones you've known.
So, I hope God will help me to keep this all in mind
And not to try and judge you or ever be unkind.
So come on in, little child
And I'll help you to unpack
And I'll do my job and love you
Till they send you back

Chapter 12

Thank God I Never Made It Past Preschool!

I NEVER HAD THE DESIRE TO WORK outside of the home and found great joy in working with little children. While many mothers couldn't wait to get beyond the bottles and diapers, I always found it to be the most enjoyable stage. I always wanted to be at home when my children got off the school bus, so home day care suited my needs. I did a lot of babysitting while my kids were young and, in 1989, I started my own in-home preschool. The first year had a mere five children enrolled in the class. My basement recreation room became a school. Word about my preschool spread rapidly and, within a few years, there were 20 children enrolled. I added another room to my school and hired a full time assistant, Leta Hubner, as well as my daughter Becky, whenever she could work in the hours after high school.

This was one of the best decisions I've ever made. It never seemed like a job. Leta and I had a connection that was unequalled. In ten years we never had that first disagreement and always respected each other's ideas. We were truly a working team. We gave the preschool 101 percent every single day. We began our day laughing and we were still laughing when the parents came to pick up their children. Sometimes I think they wondered what went on in that room below the ground!

It would take up this entire book to relate all the funny stories that we remember from this preschool. A smile still comes to our faces when we hear a certain child's name mentioned or recall an event that happened in the classroom. Likewise, we grimace at some of the stories we remember, and feel lucky that we escaped parental confrontation or intervention from Child Protective Services!

Two little sisters, Kianna and Krishana, always came to school looking like they were attending a bridal luncheon. The family was quite wealthy and the girls always wore very expensive clothing. The mother had warned us during

Santa (Dick) visits the school, without his reindeer

Time for a songfest!

orientation to never let Kianna near a pair of scissors as she had cut up all their wedding pictures and would cut up anything in sight. Well, sure enough, one day the class was all sitting around the table making a craft project that involved using scissors. When Kianna stood up, the bottom eight inches of her dress nearly fell to the floor! Fortunately her mother took the news with good grace.

On another occasion we took our preschool class on a field trip to Miller's Tree Farm. They have a pumpkin patch in the fall and it is about an hour's drive from our school. As all parents know, fresh air and then a long car ride home will soon result in an afternoon nap for a four-year-old. Several mothers drove their cars and chaperoned. We returned to school just in time for dismissal. The waiting parents all picked up their children and hurried off with pumpkins in hand to hear about their child's fun day at the pumpkin patch. Leta and I were standing around talking after school as we sometimes did, and Jessie's mother drove up to get her son. The classroom was empty and no children were to be found. After about ten minutes of frantic searching, Lisa Weast, a mother to a pair of twins in our class who had driven on the field trip, called and said she just went out to her car to retrieve something and found Jessie asleep on the floor behind the third seat of her van. Wow! How tragic that could have been!

Halloween parades, Thanksgiving feasts, visits from Santa Claus (alias our principal, Dick), lavish Easter Egg hunts, and fun field trips always filled our schedule.

Our annual end of the year field trip to Clarence Fountain's Farm

During the years of teaching preschool, I was also hired to be the birthday party hostess at McDonalds. I worked there for five years and hosted nearly 1000 parties. One day the owner/operator approached me about hosting a pre-school in the playplace. This was a great opportunity for me. No more liability in my home and no more mess to clean up each day! I jumped at the chance and we immediately filled the class by putting up a flyer in the restaurant.

Steven actually closed down the playplace to the public three afternoons a week so that we could host our pre-school. This was unheard of! The children were so excited getting to have their recess in the tubes. Our crafts and worksheets were displayed on the walls for everyone to see. They were so proud. This was an awesome set up, but like so many things in life, it was too good to be true. After one year, Steven sold his franchise; the corporation took over and said, "NO MORE PRE-SCHOOL!"

I had never worked for anyone who had as much confidence in my abilities as Steven did. He let me work out of my home scheduling parties and gave me a monthly budget to use in purchasing prizes and games for the parties.

I also wrote a book in poetry form to be presented to each child who booked a birthday party. Steven had them published at his expense and we gave them out at the parties. Steven did his best to get a copyright on the book so that we could get the royalties. However, the corporation took over my book idea, changed the wording somewhat, and sold it in their catalog as their book. We got burned!!

I wrote almost all of our finger plays and songs and today, now that Leta and I are both retired, the two of us, along with our husbands, go biking whenever we can get together, which is never often enough. We will be riding along the bike path singing our little preschool songs and our husbands just shake their heads in disbelief!

At the end of our school year, we always had lavish graduations with caps and gowns and gave a program for family and friends that we had worked on for weeks until the children had it perfected.

Field Trip to my son Skip's woodworking shop

Even though the children moved on and all graduated from high school, thank goodness Leta and I never made it past preschool! Thanks for the memories, Leta. You're the greatest. I love you.

Graduation day!

Trails of the Farmer's Daughter

Now that's a scary bunch!

Chapter 13

The Darkest Day, April 22, 2004

THE HARDEST CHAPTER TO WRITE in this book is a farewell to one of the most wonderful, inspirational, and devoted husbands and fathers who ever lived: my beloved Richard Dean Sturgeon. My children respected this man and looked up to him as if he was their God. I will never come close to gaining the respect and love my kids had for their dad. The children always knew that if they had a problem or needed financial assistance, their dad would always come through.

Dick and I were approaching our retirement years and were looking forward to our time together. We had been wintering in Myrtle Beach, South Carolina, for several years after Dick's retirement after working for 30 years at Eli Lilly. I was the only one in the family who got to see the real joy and relaxation he felt whenever he was with his golfing buddies in Myrtle Beach. A different air came about him whenever we were there. He was relaxed, had no work to do, just time to have fun. He had made lifetime retirement friends with three other golfers, Coop, Butthead, and Ter. Together they made an awesome foursome! They would golf every day during the winter months and were looking forward to having us move to Myrtle Beach. In the evenings, the guys would take their women out to dinner together, and sit at the table roaring in laughter while reminiscing about their day of golf. Dick was exhilarated every day in Myrtle Beach.

The last six months we spent in Battle Ground, Dick had a calendar where he would cross off each day in anticipation of our move. While packing a few days before his death, Dick made the comment, "I can't wait to get the hell out of here." That day never came, but Hell did.

Four days before we were to relocate to South Carolina, Dick was planning to baby-sit the grandchildren overnight. Skip and Amy were flying to a woodworking clinic in North Carolina. I was busy packing and cleaning our home on Tenskwatawa Drive so that we could move to Myrtle Beach the following week. Dick decided to wing it alone but I told him to call me in the morning when he was ready for me to relieve him so that he could make his 10:30 tee time at The Elks Country Club.

Last picture of Dick, taken while we were packing to move

The last conversation I had with Dick was on Wednesday night. He told me he loved me and said, "Don't work too hard, Sweatheart." (This is not a misprint, Dick always called me 'Sweatheart' because I was always on the move!) He said he'd call me in the morning when the children got up to tell me how his night of babysitting went.

Thursday morning came and Dick had not gotten back to me. Then around 10 a.m. his golfing buddies started calling our house from The Elks asking, "Where's Sturg?" I assumed that Dick was overwhelmed with his job of Mr. Mom and time had just gotten away. Then, about 20 minutes later, his golfing buddy, Russ Barrick, called again and asked, "Has Sturg called yet? I guess we'll just have to start without him."

Golfing was so important to Dick that I knew he wouldn't just leave his buddies hanging. There must be some kind of problem. I told Russ I would jump in the car and go see what the holdup was.

As I walked into Skip's house, something just didn't seem right. Dick's Ford Explorer was sitting in the driveway, it was past 10:30 a.m., and the house was totally quiet. No pitter-patter of little feet, no TV playing, just a very eerie quiet.

I called Dick's name softly so as not to awaken the little ones, ages three and five. I then walked into the family room and the heaviest, most sickening feeling came over me that I have ever felt. Our entire life, and our future together, flashed in front of my eyes. Something even I cannot explain. Everything was gone. I too, felt as if I had died. I knew before I ever walked across the room that Dick was dead. I kept hollering from a distance, "Don't do this to me! We have our whole future ahead of us. Wake up! This can't be happening!"

I paced the floor, tearing at my hair, rubbing my eyes, and hoping to wake up from this horrible nightmare. Then I touched his cold body and knew that he was gone.

I had just buried my aunt, uncle, nephew, mother, and father within the past two years. My father had just died the month before. When the undertaker came to Skip's house to take the body away, I was in shock. He looked at me and said, "Oh, no, it's you again. I am so sorry."

The next few days were all a blur. I didn't know anything could hurt so badly. I had lost my first and only love, and also my best friend since childhood. To me there was no future.

We buried Dick in the Liberty Chapel Cemetery on 900 North just a few hundred yards down the road from where we'd raised our five wonderful children.

The funeral was absolutely overwhelming. Over 500 guests came to call. Dick had played Santa Claus and principal to dozens of my preschoolers over the years and many came to show their respect.

My five wonderful children taken the day of their dad's funeral. Left to right Shane, Becky, Steve, Skip, and Scott

At the funeral home, a young man with crutches and braces on his legs came slowly struggling up to Dick's casket. He looked at me and said with a smile, "Hi, Mom. It's Duke. I'm just here to tell Dad thank-you and good-bye." He was one of the foster children we had nurtured 13 years previously.

Lines wrapped around the funeral home for hours. The following day was a beautiful sunny day as we laid our hero to rest. Soller-Baker said it was one of the largest funeral processions they had ever seen. My sister flew in from California and gave the eulogy along with Reverend Donald Carpenter, the minister who had married Dick and me 39 years before. Linda gave the most inspirational and dynamic tribute that anyone could receive. I know Dick was listening and he must have felt very honored.

Food overflowed the kitchen counters and flowers were in abundance. Leta cooked non stop for 48 hours. She provided enough food for our entire family to make it through that dismal week after Dick's death.

Dick had been a Mustang Coach to hundreds of eight to ten year old boys in the summer recreation program, and had never missed one of his own son's games. He holds the record for most wins in a season by any baseball team in

Tippecanoe County. Go Battle Ground Buckles (the feed depot who sponsored the team)!

As a tribute to Dick, a memorial golf tournament has been held for many years and the proceeds are used to sponsor an underprivileged child who might not otherwise have the funding to play baseball with his friends.

A memorial rock has been placed at the entrance to the ballpark in Dick's honor. Battle Ground is a very close-knit community. Many families will be there for generations to come. In future years, people will be passing by that huge stone and will stop to recall a story about a game with the ornery "Sturg," and you can bet it will always end with a win and a smile!

Remembering my first love at "Sturg's Rock"

Chapter 14

Never Look Back

AFTER SEVERAL MONTHS OF GRIEVING in self-pity, I decided it was time to move forward and try to find peace with myself. I began performing demos (giving out samples) in local grocery stores and Wal-Mart, to help fill my days. By fate, my boss had also lost her husband three years prior to my becoming a widow and many times when she would call to schedule me for a demo, we would talk and cry for nearly an hour. Even though I had never met her in person, she was like a therapist to me.

I was so lost. Before Dick died, I had never driven outside of Lafayette, never balanced a checkbook, or deposited or withdrawn money from a bank. I did know that taxes had to be paid by April 15th, but had no knowledge of how to prepare them. The reason I knew the deadline was because Dick was like me and always hated to part with his money. He would wait until the last minute to prepare his taxes and we always found ourselves taking a ride into Lafayette around 11 p.m. on April 15th to drop the envelope in the mailbox at the main post office so that it could be postmarked by midnight.

I will be forever grateful to Shane for his guidance and wisdom of knowing how to invest and figure out all of the financial mess after Dick died so suddenly. Our family agreed to give him power of attorney and he stepped in and handled my finances beautifully.

The morning of January 16, 2005, not quite nine months after Dick passed away, I was scheduled to work at Wal-Mart. This guy came up to my demo table and began talking. He had lost his wife to cancer in April, 2004, the same month I had lost Dick. He had been married 39 years, the same as me. He asked if I'd like to go out dancing sometime and I told him I wasn't ready. We continued to talk awhile and before leaving, he picked up a napkin off the table and we exchanged phone numbers. As he walked away, I took a deep breath and said to myself, "Lord, what have I done?"

From that moment on, I couldn't get this guy off my mind. All my neighbors and girlfriends said I had a glow about me that they had never seen before. My sister in California could tell by the tone of my voice that something good had happened. When I called to tell her that I had found someone, she said, "I already know!"

My sister said that Nancy, Ray's deceased wife, and Dick, my deceased husband, were sitting on a cloud one day looking down from heaven and decided it was time to make their move and make the two of us happy once again. She may be right.

For the first time since Dick's death, I felt like my life wasn't over. But things just seemed to be happening too fast. I began to feel guilty—like I was cheating on Dick. Ray left dozens of phone messages on my answering machine but I never returned his calls. He was not about to give up and remained determined for two months.

I waited until Dick had been gone for a full year and finally agreed to meet Ray on neutral ground and walk the ocean. The rest was history. From our very first meeting, I knew that this was the guy I'd like to live out my senior years with. He was very patient with me and we spent many hours talking and sharing memories of our loved ones. We understood each other and cherished the value of a good marriage.

Ray's wife Nancy was only 55 when she died of multiple sclerosis and cancer, and Dick was only 59 when he had a massive heart attack. It reminds me of a plaque I now have hanging in my kitchen at the lake, "Be thankful you are growing older. It is a privilege denied to many."

When together, Ray and I felt like we had so much to offer each other. We picked each other up when we were down. We began laughing and enjoying life. We were like two teenagers in love!

Then on Valentine's Day, February 14, 2007, Ray invited me down to his oceanfront condo for dinner. When I approached the building, a guy was standing on the top balcony waving his arms with a huge banner that said, "Will you marry me?"

I ran up to the room and Ray greeted me at the door with a ring box in his hand. After he proposed and I said "yes," we headed down to Cowboys, our favorite country dancing spot and celebrated the occasion with our friends.

Ray was the second man I had ever dated in my life. Call it luck or call it fate, but I have been blessed to have been loved by two of the most wonderful and caring men on earth.

We were married out on the oceanfront in Myrtle Beach, SC, in front of the M Grand Hotel on December 29, 2007, but not without avail.

We were to be married at noon. Taking the advice of my good friend, Mary Seitz, we kept everything very simple and inexpensive. She had sent me a note a few weeks earlier to see how my wedding plans were progressing. She said, "Just remember to K.I.S.S." (Keep It Simple, Stupid). Well, we did our part by keeping it simple, and the minister did his part by being stupid. He didn't even show up at the wedding!

The music was playing and 80 guests were waiting for us to make our grand entrance out onto the beach. My sister came bolting into the hotel room where I was putting on the finishing touches and dramatically announced, "Now, Sandie, don't get upset. We have a little problem. The minister hasn't shown up yet!"

Of course, I was a basket case and burst into tears. My sister, being the optimist that she is, ran down to the lobby to get a phone book and call the Chapel by the Sea.

In the meantime, I'm sitting on the bed, crying uncontrollably as my sister-in-law Donna, who had flown in from Indiana, is telling me it's going to be okay. Friends and family from eight different states had come to witness this special day.

Linda had her bouquet in hand when she stepped into the elevator. A black lady said, "Oh, you must be here for a wedding." Linda said, "Well we were, but the minister didn't show up."

The lady quickly responded, "I'm a minister!" My sister said, "Don't leave, come with me." Linda brought the minister, Reverend Santasha Cooper to our hotel room and once again reminded me that Dick and Nancy were up on a cloud looking out for us!

Reverend Cooper sat Ray and I down on the bed in the hotel room and counseled us for a few minutes on the commitment of marriage. We told her our stories and she agreed to marry us.

When we finally appeared out on the beach 30 minutes late, our family and friends were cheering us on more like we'd just won a marathon rather than being united in marriage. Looking back, I think they were right!

All of our seven children and ten grandchildren in this new blended family were there to witness this happy occasion. It took a lot of coordinating but we accomplished our goal. Unfortunately, this has been the only time during our married life that all of our family has gotten together.

Ray and I with our entire family on our wedding day

As we begin to age, and each day is the same as the next, hopefully we'll all remember this special day, as it was also Ray's 65th birthday. On every anniversary, I remind him that he'll never again get a birthday gift as great as that one!

I also like to remind him that I got him at Wal-Mart, and the sign above the door reads, "Satisfaction guaranteed or your money back." Do I feel really secure about this marriage!

Not too long ago, my good friend Mary Seitz, sent a letter and said, "Aren't you glad that Ray came along that day at Wal-Mart to sample your stuff?" Isn't it funny how a good friend can read your mind?

Satisfaction guaranteed!

Chapter 15

A Cold Nose Can Feel So Warm!

It wouldn't seem quite right to write a book on my life without mentioning the most loyal and cheapest therapist one could ever have.

Three years before Dick passed away; we were starting to look forward to retirement and were spending a month in Myrtle Beach each winter. This seemed like the perfect retirement location as Dick was an avid golfer and the sunshine suited me perfectly.

While wintering there in 2001, I had way too much time on my hands to shop while Dick was out golfing every day with his buddies. The Myrtle Beach Flea Market became a very popular spot for me to get exercise and fill my days. One Saturday, a lady with a litter of six-week-old Maltese puppies had set up a booth and was trying to sell them to those with the softest hearts! There were three in the litter, two females and one little male, and I do mean little. He was the runt of the litter and weighed 15 ounces. Having been a foster mother for most of my nurturing years, I knew how to take a nearly starving, frail newborn and make him or her blossom with a little food, love, and attention. I couldn't get that puppy out of my mind. I whined and begged Dick for several days, questioning him as to "Why can't I buy that cute little ball of white fur?"

For two weeks, Dick kept telling me that we didn't need another dog, as we already had one back in Indiana. Little did I know that Dick had already gone back and purchased the puppy for me, but the breeder wouldn't release him to come home until he weighed one pound!

I had almost given up hope of getting my Maltese until one morning Dick came walking into the condo with a very small Burger King sack, all folded down nicely, and announced, "Here's your breakfast!" I opened the sack and down inside were these two little black eyes staring up at me through a little mound of white fur! This was so typical of Dick. He delighted in teasing people and acting tough, but inside he had a heart of gold and always strived to make me happy. Dick had only one request. We must name the puppy "Bogey." Dick loved the whole Myrtle Beach golfing scene and, unknown to me, this was a golf term meaning one over par. I never asked Dick what he paid for Bogey, but he always said it was way over par!

Bogey

Bogey immediately became one of the family. He was a great traveler and made numerous trips between Indiana and Myrtle Beach.

After Dick passed away, even three years later, Bogey would stand on the sofa, peering across the golf course, and would bark excessively whenever he saw a golfer similar to Dick's build. He would get so excited when someone would come to the door towards evening. It took a long time for Bogey to realize that daddy was not coming home.

I don't know how I could have coped with life after Dick's death without Bogey by my side. I was forced to move to Myrtle Beach four days after I buried my husband. I was alone in a new home with no furnishings, and I didn't even know my way to the grocery store. I would pull over to the side of the road and cry. For months, I didn't leave the house, get out of my pajamas, or eat a healthy meal. Bogey would lie beside me in bed all day long. The term "faithful companion" certainly held true with this dog.

After awhile he forced me to get up, get dressed, and start my day. The only fresh air I got was from walking the dog.

Bogey stayed loyal to his breed, the Maltese Lap Dog. He was continually in my lap whenever I would sit and cry and look out the window at the golfers and scream, "This isn't fair! Dick is supposed to be out there with your foursome!" "How dare you even drive your golf carts past my door!" "Stop laughing and having a good time." "Shouldn't you be grieving over the loss of my husband?" This stage of my anger went on for nearly a year.

I went into a state of depression and rarely ate. I would look at the empty chair across the table from me and literally fall apart. I nearly became anorexic. One day I became so weak that I passed out in the bathroom and awoke later lying between the stool and the wall. Sure enough, as soon as I came to, Bogey was there, licking my face!

In 2005 when I met that wonderful man named Ray Uptegrove, I wasn't ready to begin a relationship so I wouldn't tell Ray where I lived. Being that I'm from the old school, I didn't realize that through working with a computer and a GPS, nearly everyone can be found today. One day I saw a note attached to my front door. It said, "Sorry I missed you. You have a very cute dog. Call me sometime. Ray."

After two months, I called Ray but told him that my dog and I come as a package deal; you get me, you get my dog! Luckily, Ray was a dog lover and he and his wife had always had one.

We began taking Bogey everywhere. Ray and Bogey became good buddies. Ray would put Bogey in the back hatch of his kayak and paddle him out to Waite Island where Bogey would run to his heart's content. Ray would put Bogey in his "see through" mesh backpack and bike all over Myrtle Beach. The little old ladies along the bike path would stop him and say, "Oh how cute! Is that a real dog in your backpack?" It wasn't very long until Ray was referring to Bogey as his "pick-up dog"!

Through the years, we had many near-tragic experiences with Bogey but somehow always got him reconnected with the family.

Once, while on a two and a half month camping trip, we lost Bogey in Vancouver, Washington. We were there visiting Scott and Heather. Somehow, Bogey escaped through the cat trap door in the garage. When we returned, Bogey was gone! We all were frantically going up and down the streets in the neighborhood, calling his name. Within a few minutes, several neighbors had also joined the search. I was about to give up hope and was crying uncontrollably. We had to leave Washington the next morning and I was not about to leave without my dog. Then suddenly a woman came strolling out of her house with this very clean, well-groomed, white dog and said, "Are you looking for a dog?" She had found Bogey walking down the street, hungry, wet and dirty, and had taken him into her home and given him a bath.

The next incident caused a near separation in our relationship. Bogey loved riding in the back hatch of Ray's kayak but I was always fearful that he could fall out and drown. Ray always reassured me that "the dog isn't going anywhere!" Then one day while kayaking on Canandaigua Lake in New York, I was paddling way ahead and Ray was leisurely paddling along behind me. I hollered back and said, "How's Bogey doing?" Ray said, "Okay." A few minutes later, I looked back and said, "Where's Bogey?" Unbeknown to Ray, the poor dog had fallen out of the kayak and was swimming frantically, trying to catch up with the boat. We circled around and picked up a very tired and soggy dog. I gave Ray the silent treatment the rest of the day.

Bogey was ten years old in 2011 and I hope that he is still with us when I finally get around to finishing this book. He's been through major hernia repair surgery and, at every annual checkup, the veterinarian cannot believe he is still alive. He has literally become our little boy. He has lived in four homes with us and traveled thousands of miles in the car and camper. While traveling from place to place, I always remind Ray, "Don't forget the baby!" — like we ever could. Every time we pack the car, Bogey is standing in the doorway, wagging his tail and giving us those sad puppy eyes, just waiting to hear the words, "Let's go!"

When evening falls, Bogey begins pacing the floor and dropping his stuffed animals at our feet, trying to get us to go to bed with him. Ray is always the first one to oblige.

Then I go through the nightly routine, much like reading a bedtime story to a child. "Are you warm enough?" "Do you want a drink of water?" "Would you like a little treat?" Ray's eyebrows raise, his eyes light up, but then he finally realizes that I'm actually just talking to the dog!

In Closing

I'VE TRIED TO LEAVE A LEGACY for my children by writing the stories of my life and my heritage. Even though they may not be interested at the moment, perhaps the day will come when they will want to pick up this book and maybe even add a few chapters about their own life to keep the tradition going.

As I read through my book, I cannot believe how quickly life completes its cycle. The fact that my entire life can be consolidated into one small book is actually quite scary!

Losing my husband at such a young age was a real wake-up call. My advice to the younger generation is to enjoy each day to its fullest as you never know what tomorrow may bring. Since I began writing this book two years ago (2010), cataracts have tried to rob me of my sight, scoliosis is trying to cripple me, and cancer is trying to invade my body. I'm trying to take care of myself, as life has not handed me the simple little package that I thought I was going to receive. Just think about what you would do if this were your last day on earth and then proceed to do it!

Try to see a positive side of every negative situation you find yourself involved with. Looking back, I remember all those days after Dick's death that I was too depressed to even get up and get dressed—but at least I didn't have to make the bed! My world nearly crumbled beneath me but now I am slowly rebuilding a new life for myself, my new husband, and my family. We travel between New York, Myrtle Beach, Florida, and Indiana. While trying to find a place to call home, a voice inside me keeps calling me back to Indiana. I love and miss all my children and grandchildren, but they are literally scattered all over the world. I will never be able to live close to all of them, but a house is just a house. Creating memories inside is what makes it a home. I just hope that wherever I settle and live out my senior years, my family will always be greeted at my door with a smile and a hug, and always get the feeling of "coming home."

An Ending Poem to Ponder…

As I look back upon my life
I find both joy and pain
And know not to wait for the storm to pass
But learn to dance in the rain.

For life can throw you some curve balls
But you still can win the game
If you learn to look forward instead of back
When things are never the same.

So to my future generations
Please take the time to look
At all the blessings bestowed on you
By reading Sandie's book.

God bless you all

Sandie

To order additional copies of this book contact
Rancho Lazarus Publications via
www.rancholazarus.com